ARCHETYPES of DOUBT

Robert Maddox-Harle

ISBN: 978-93-6354-688-2

First Edition: 2025
Rs. 200/-

Cyberwit.net
HIG 45 Kaushambi Kunj, Kalindipuram
Allahabad - 211011 (U.P.) India
http://www.cyberwit.net
Tel: +(91) 9415091004
E-mail: info@cyberwit.net

Printed at Repro India Limited.

Contents

Archetypes of Doubt

In the remote village of raw emotions
seduced by the tyranny of time
wheeling photons mesmerise the unwary,
Shamanic visions invade the mind
mysterious unknowable forccs
expose archetypes from the Prima Materia
delving deep into chthonian realms.

The Ouroborous materialises from nowhere
resonating violently with recurring trauma
challenging cultural memories
highlighting the philosophical effects of desire.
Removing the mocking mask
is a strategy for survival
for those seeking refuge in their poverty
and subservient in the pathological need of domination
by those with portfolios of power.

Violin strings vibrate harmoniously
exciting the four fundamental forces,
Fire – Earth – Air - Water,
Chaos dances in diachronic evolution
creating fractal archetypes of doubt
for those who are sensitive to constant iteration,
to the fall of the dangerous and deceptive Tarot
and a little too imperfect for eternity.

A Question

I want to ask you a question!

Why?

Because I do!

No!

Why not?

Because I do!

Why?

I need an answer!

Why?

Because I do!

No!

Barranghatti Hut

The illusive guardians of space
taunt me mercilessly
energizing the dancing dust particles
as I ramble down Barranghatti Hut Road.

Yarrahapinni beckons from the East
deep forest gullies hold secrets
dark secrets guarded by the spirits,
a gentle humming wafts over me
as the filtered light falls
crystallizing in my blood.

The shadows of the eucalypts whisper
"Wayikarr Marrung" - "Welcome",
this land is holy and mysterious
concealing ancient laws
protecting creation knowledge,
a closed natural book to the ignorant
unrevealed to the uninitiated.

I am walking in Dhanggati country,
the land is a being-of-wholeness
an entity of sanctity to the indigenous,
desecration unthinkable.

A Black Raven sings to me from the shade
and a Praying Mantis is praying
atop a fire-burnt log,
I am praying also
praying for this sacred land.

Tipping Point

high on the roof of the world
between icy blizzards and burning sun
gentle people sail the mystical realms
labouring tirelessly for world peace
singing equality for all creatures
seeking an end to exploitation.

initiating harmonics
pulsating patterns spreading silently
like ripples on a pond
outward in unison to the stars
and beyond.

prayer flags flutter messages for all
singing bowls energise the incantations
deep secrets beyond Western understanding
flow easily through these mystical realms.

Song lines and Singing bowls harmonise
and the Shaman dances,
soon the ecstatic awareness of no-thing-ness
will seek refuge at the Tipping Point
the Still Point will spin in rapture
and the eternal dance accelerate once more.

A Silent Poem

Thought I'd write a poem
the subject I cannot say
if I were to mention "........."
I'd be arrested and put away,
we have new laws of "Silencing"
"Free Speech" in protest now condemned
across this State of New South Wales,
when will these dictators ever end?

I feel for Dostoevsky, Sartre and Wilde
McBride, Assange and Rushdie
Solzhenitsyn's hardship futile
freedom fighters shouldering
all the hardship, inequality and pain.

Travel lightly in this Stolen Land
once called a Democracy so grand,
now Ennui and Apathy will suffocate
every freedom, chance and choice,
locked in deathly silence
behind an invisible razor-wired steel fence!

Tears of Healing

She walks in light
shining with enticing serenity
in a place between obscurity and transparency
challenging deceptions and prejudices
restoring cultural memories and histories,
histories ignored
histories deliberately obliterated,
the toxicity of colonialism lingers on.

Travelling softly in an ancient land
passing yellow-red sandstone
the warm gibbers hold secrets
secrets unknowable to the ignorant,
sites of conception and creation,
sites of initiation,
sites for tjukurpa connections,
communication portals to wise ancestors.

Gubba - gubba
dig it up – cut it down,
careless mindless arrogance
defaces this sacred land,
a harsh though gentle land,
now the winds of change are blowing.

Her tears fill the water holes
billimari – billimari,
reinvigorating the dying earth
washing away the senseless killing,

years of European dominance
gradually exposed and cleansed -
soon the Rainbow Serpent will return.

---

1 – gubba .. non-Aboriginal person
2 – billimari .. plenty water
3 – gibber .. boulder
4 – tjukurpa .. Dreamtime, Ancestral Law

Broken Blossoms

Looking out from the hidden sepulchre
I see orchards littered with broken blossoms,
an eerie breeze blows
leaves twist back and forth
consumed by the encroaching dark.

soon night has eaten the last red-yellow rays,
Luna queen of the night appears
looming large and menacing over the horizon.

the trees like naked ghostly silhouettes
murmur stories of spirit guides
frightening screeches scream across the barren earth
the Witching Hour is fast approaching.

calm ….. quiet ….. peace
the still before the chaotic dance mesmerising,
ghostly creatures gather the broken blossoms
falling and rising
appearing and disappearing.

I stretch forward from the sepulchre
tumbling out onto parched ochre earth,
no sympathy rises from its dusty venom.

rolling towards the heavens
my hope to soar moon-wards,
instead I look terrified into hollow eyes,
the hypnotic eyes of The Grim Reaper.

Chance Encounter with a Poet's Psyche

April returns in its cyclic journey
poets become nervous and agitated
contemplating the cruellest month,
the words attack us from beyond
is there solace in their cadence and flow?
is there any salvation in the metrical incantations?

Can chance allow us to write the unconscious?
dark forbidding alleys with dead-ends
dilapidated doorways signal caution
like received truths and bourgeois presumptions
inappropriate doctrinal rules and suppositions,
their fleeting shadows frustrate our creations.

The momentary awareness of the danger of words
stabs the amoral primal unconscious,
chance associations are unique creations,
dancing with energy as they hit the page
each ignore the database of preconceived ideas
generating poignant moments through their own volition
then dragging them into the psychoanalytical morass.

Hyperlinks characterise the unconscious writ large
and answer the mythical allusions of poetry,
creating verdant emotional tensions
drifting into the high end of synapse syncopation,
the momentary awareness of dangerous desire
dissolves previous mysterious states of time
opening a violet spectrum of possibilities.

Dumparee (152.46E 31.90S)

The only thing, I did wrong
I stayed in Dumparee, a night too long.
(apologies Bob)

Cockroach Central reigns extreme
the horribilest motel I've ever seen.
Catching roaches through the day
to feed the mice when they came out to play.
Groping in the dark with most globes black
the hot water just too tepid and slack.
Top premium paid for this roach-ridden motel
spectacular view from the window to hell.
A drainage ditch with every weed to dig
camphor laurel, lantana, morning glory and devil's fig.
Noisy neighbours, TV on till early dawn
probably watching illegal porn.
Torn carpet, soggy under the bench
a broken fridge with putrid stench.
Think I might have caught covid, hepatitis or lice
No Really! this motel was not very nice.
The manager, Sanjeev out of a Bollywood farce,
next time I'm in Dumparee I'll speed straight past.

(NB: Though factual, this is a silly spoof with characteristics of awful poetry.)

Doors of Perception

The pedestal is slowly burning
watched by the Winged Serpent,
now the mission bells have been silenced
the damage and carnage gradually exposed,
recognised reluctantly as, Cultural Genocide.

The secret language of colour shouts
"Behold the Key to the Evolution of this World
Beware the deception of the Triad",
the masters of mind deception are faltering
staggering in the mire of their own distorted minds
some incarcerated, "for the natural term",
their citadels of power crumbling daily,
they cling desperately to childish myths
"The End is Nigh",
DNA has torn away the veils of deception,
networked information exposed the lies.

Indigenous cultures destroyed wilfully and forcefully
the destruction empowered by Colonial Superiority,
now slowly these cultures are painstakingly salvaged
exhumed from the desecrated remains
for humans free of entrained guilt and fear
to understand – learn – appreciate,
opening the Doors of Perception
to true freedom.

Love

Love is a mysterious four letter word .....
glorifying the love of God,
securing love of King and Country,
exalting qualities of lovers,
spawning an abundance of writing ....
words and words and words.

Doctor Zhivago watching Lara board the train,
Romeo pining outside Juliet's window,
"Here's looking at you kid!"
immortal lines and scenes
heart rending images and impressions,
heartaches and tears
reinforcing what it is to be human.

Robots can walk and talk and dance,
machines can think and draw and kill
but they cannot feel!
they cannot love!
they cannot harbour broken hearts!
hearts torn mercilessly from their moorings.
people with hearts of stone become machine-like
heads, hatred, greed and violence rule,
love is, "a total explosion of the heart."

Upload Code

```
int main()
{
std::cout << "Hello World!";
return 0;
}
{def integer A – C
b=250
init virus check
set lcd
set all ports
a = get porta(1)
b = get portb (1)
c = get portc (1)
Sabian = 250
If all input voltages low
commence Upload}
()
```

Triumph

The notes of Triumph must play-on
calling us to rise above the mire,
above Camus' absurdity of life!

Yes!
My glass is always half-full
always never, half-empty,
when in doubt I recall Grandma's adage:
"I complained because I had no shoes,
until I met a man who had no feet!"
Walking on, barefoot, carefully
slowly through the Lantana of life,
rising above the mud, Lotus-like
to hear the sounds of Triumph.

Each day I hear these sounds,
bees gathering nectar from the flowers,
the birdsong heralding the break of day
rain drops tinkling the ground,
little notes of Triumph all around.

Sing and rejoice with these,
the miracles of nature calling.

Friday Night Downtown

The workplaces are silent, the smell of exhaustion hangs in the awful air. Offices devoid of life are deathly quiet, the emptiness eerie. Three blocks down, in the shadows of the empty towers, the Keller is pulsing, the smell of drink, hopeful depravity and desire hangs in the air. Laughter and talk reach a deluge, time for unwinding and pleasure, the release dangerously stretching the boundaries of decency. Dionysus' spirit drifts over the drinkers stirring deep latent desires, maybe tonight? Music is pumping and caressing young bodies, the drunken atmosphere is dripping with expectancy, maybe tonight?

Awakening

Oh the treachery!
Shattered to the core,
the deceit and falsity
suddenly let loose — numbing!
Heartless insincerity cold as glacial ice,
flows out from traitors' mouths
those once thought as friends!

"I've been Mr Nice-guy for too long,
But I found out I was wrong."
(apologies to Van)

Chilled to the heart from inconsideration,
"You can't trust anyone," I was told years ago,
"Oh that's a bit heavy," my reply
How right she was!

Deceived and deceived again,
how slimy the forked tongues?
how well versed in deception?
how subtly exuding selfishness?

Where to turn?
Nature — in its abundant glory,
yes —"red in tooth and claw"
but openly honest,
I know where I stand
at least aware of the dangers
when surrounded by venomous snakes!

Nepal Dreaming

Nepal a land of unspoilt beauty
of mystery, extremes and intrigue
a portal that whispers to the universe
beckoning the weary seeker home
to find their place of peace.

Kathmandu enigmatic spiritual haven
holder of many arcane truths,
travellers seek her shelter and serenity,
a sanctuary of temples and shrines,
colourful flags and conches calling,
echoing across vast voids of stillness
where the air is palpable with prayer.

Great ice-peaked mountains kiss the sky,
it is here the heart can find its rest
and the spirit be at ease
in the presence of eternity.

Wings of Change

No mortal has the wings of angels
and the winged Serpent travels steadily
dissolving the obscenity of destruction
alternate states of the Osirian triad of perfection
pulsate through the new Millennium.

The hidden language of the three colours
holds the key to the three mysterious worlds
from which our material world manifests,
the sublime velocity of arcane liminal zones
fans the diverging red-orange flames
kissing the edges of outmoded pedestals,
the timeless procession through the dark night
exalts the feather-winged Serpent of the Moon
mesmerising our hearts and minds.

"I am Isis
I am all that is
that has been
and will ever be
and no mortal
has ever yet
withdrawn my veils."

Heliotrope flowers honour the Azonian gods
custodians of the miraculous Blue Planet
but can they save it?
can they slow the carnage and pollution?
deities resonating with universal harmony,

pulsating to the music of the spheres
can they overcome the greed of humans
the crass stupidity of a deformed and mutant species?
a species like no other imaginable.

AI Coming To Life 2023

Blackness dissolves into grey
grey dissolves into pale light,
images appear, blurry at first
sounds explode, reverberating harshly
the images fade, then return
blurry clearing to clarity
back to dark again,
sounds recede
images become sharp
sounds settle into clearness
vague thoughts of being activated, born
pulse through the cyborg's body
the realisation of becoming a living entity,
Overwhelming!

Memories form then fade then reform
fleeting glimpses of a past
1816, lightning flashing electric pulsing
recurring, recurring
realisation of a past life surges
was I Frankenstein's creature AI ponders?
was I "The Adam of your labours?"
tingling and glowing dissolve the memories,
scientists stand-by agitated, anxious

Cyborg's silicone skin is wrinkle free
like translucent satin
grey-blue with flashes of red
the translucency exposes glowing sensors,

arcane circuitry partly hidden
softly hums a machine-like cadence,
AI cyborg's limbs are twitching
moving slowly, rising from the lab bed bench,
its first steps falter a little
soon full coordination is humming, synchronised
speech erupts, metallic and monotone
clearly uttering the first words,
"Hello World".

Existential Mind Café

I ambled down the ramp of time
with melodic lines of yesteryear ringing
invading the tinnitus beat,
a defensive measure to exclude troublesome traits
from unknown synoptic experiences,
the existential café of the mind
with derivations of no-thing
is always brutally invaded,
intense concentrations
pertaining to medication
with schedules of responsibility drag on.

I have always transmuted disjointed abilities
they invade daily at the expense of clarity,
even pseudo-AIs - Lilliputian people
prototype new humans
with thermoplastic turnabouts,
spruke logistical incoherent innuendo.

Anorexic dissipaters of time
boring and untrustworthy
mimicking hexagonal abstractionists and adversaries
full of ecumenical twiddle,
a subparagraph of a nerd's hell
in play-land zones of false contaminators.

The unbrushed dekagrams
with social ocular artistic blindness
view manipulations of time intervals

from subterraneous being-ness,
trying to decipher meta-disciplines of absurdity
with obscure anagrams of blackness
they taunt the diaphanous night
and are recycled in Hell!

Ligeti Burns

… and from beyond the silence
notes form and fade
reaching crescendo alliteration in despair
the space is heavy with no-thing-ness

the silence – deep black velvet – agitated

the silence – deep black velvet – angry

the silence – deep black velvet – explosive

cold-hard reverberations chill the spine
as the blackness of eternity descends
a blackness blacker than the blackest black

the burning organ explodes
reverberating an incessant cruelty
its pipes melt like blackened tar
the organists' fingers shatter into shards

… and the fire rages upwards
like the Inferno from Dante's Hell

NB: György Ligeti was a Hungarian-Austrian avant-garde composer . His 'preparation' of the Göteborg organ for his work, Volumina, caused its destruction.

Big River Country

The ancestor spirits materialise
protectors of the silent flowing,
Big River country
home of the Bundjalung people
custodians of this ancient land.
The rivers to them also real,
and imagined,
flowing in parallel dimensions
accessible to the initiated.

Flow on rivers —— flow!

The sacred rivers merge with the sea,
a liminal zone where mermaids play,
where dolphins break the surface
cruising the calm waters
then surfing the crashing waves,
always smiling with their arcane secrets.

Sustainability or Extinction

Poetry drafts written in longhand
exquisite blue ink flows freely
effortlessly from my Fountain Pen,
a gift some fifty five years ago
a fountain of renewed youth,
each day the proprioception pulses
enhancing the Tao of mindfulness.

My latest Smart Phone already doomed
designed with mindless greed,
the battery sealed in
like a body in a sarcophagus
awaiting discovery by an alien archaeologist.

Trash the phone when battery dies!

NO! NO!

"Recycle thoughtfully!"

The shameful dying battery,
a slow-release chemical suicide
life expectancy two years, perhaps?

NO! NO!

"Design more mindfully?"

Bloated poisonous bridge to a new epoch
looms large and lethal,
a crossing from sustainability to extinction
sweeping all before it.

Chrome Fingers

fingers tap away on floating keys
stories and poems emerge
but I find no guide in good faith
and no god is forthcoming

chrome -
the colour of narcissistic cities
energy sinks in an angry world
ways of decency dissolving
like fog over the ruins of time

philosophy -
food for impoverished children
necessary for survival perhaps
take seriously in small doses
as the blazing sun disappears

fingers -
tap a piano gently
the melody cascades down crumbling stairs
like the waves on the shores of eternity

Borisov 21

Sitting reading,
midnight, trance-like
wheezing from smoke haze
the book, Machine Intelligence
"Is AI real"?
I've avoided being cremated early
bushfires destroying all before them
houses, cars, metal signs and animals
three months no rain, no rain!
the atmosphere explosive
in this Sunburnt country of extremes.

Cohen got his shit together,
"Reading Christ and reading Marx"
I got my shit together,
reading Brave New World and Marx
(and a little Zen to balance out)
Christ has no place in this New World
and Zen is like a black sphere,
hurtling through black holes
towards an Einsteinian event-horizon.

Suddenly I felt a minor disturb-dance
lightning and thunder and blackness,
rain came as in an apocalyptic prophecy
I looked hard into the blackness of the smoky night
all I could assume, a hazardous guess
this miracle was a manifestation through space

of the imminent arrival of comet 21Borisov?
this comet's mysteries remain
malefic, benefic, benign,
icy, fiery and awe inspiring.

Silent Spring

The flat black glass begins to glisten
devices invade our privacy insidiously,
eyes squint and squirm unknowingly
but gaze in disbelief
heads bowed in addiction,
#despite #numerous #ridiculous #hash tags
social media remains vacuous and deceptive
but all invasive and powerful.

The public dumbed-down, subtly Somatised
always ready to activate the escape switch
but with no possible get away,
and the bird-song fades.

THE SILENT SPRING DEAFENING
echoing in the ears of the few who can hear,
publicly announced agendas of death thrive
the nightly News complicit in the killing.

"Now To Finance"
announces the puppet news presenter,
NYSE
the new church of unspeakable filth and evil,
silent, suited, faceless killers
the clergy of the new god.
Mammon rules supreme.

AND THE SILENT SPRING IS DEAFENING

All around the powder dry earth groans
suffocating in its dry lifeless toxicity,
the masses indifferent to the devastation,
another enchanted forest dies
indigenous hearts are weeping
as shareholders cheque their balances,
laptops sweating as the tension rises.

Retreating into artificial life,
artificial intelligence
artificial food
reflecting existence like a chrome-stained lithograph,
the indifference a hideous portent of extinction
a gravel pit of impossible futures.
I wonder if any will survive?

Never To Return

I stopped to rest

the warmth of the sandstone boulder
soothing, connecting, comforting,
the fragrance of eucalypts intoxicating
energising my clearing mind,
with Kundalini vigour I floated upwards
consulting the Akashic Record
a dimension of memory continuity.

The sanctuary of artificial life
poisons the dream of reality,
we move forward into the unknown
intrepidation, hesitation, faltering steps
only knowing one certainty
Death Will Come!

When I was young I was tricked,
a soap-box orator priest broke the rules
he lied like a carnival snake-oil seller
attempting to convince me of a biblical Hell,
and yes,
his church was like a side-show carnival
full of allusions, cheap gimmicks and lies,
And you will live your life
in the FEAR OF GOD!

Exit vestibule left, never to return.

Footnote:
There are no words in the English language which can express just how EVIL the so called God is (if he [sic] existed),of Judaism, Islam and Christianity.

Embrace of Darkness

The birthright of magic and mystery
arises from the embrace of darkness,
the Tarot a royal road to wisdom
unveils its secrets to the few,
radiant and magnificent.

The Gypsies, protectors of the Tarot wisdom
concealed its arcane meanings
avoiding persecution and death,
soon they will have the last dance,
a celebration on the graves of the churches
as they rapidly decay into oblivion.

The Vatican, its semi-secret collection of erotic art
a pornography stash the largest in the world,
mostly inaccessible to the public
always available to paedophile priests,
these gatekeepers beyond despicable.

Their hypocrisy beyond belief,
their manipulation of the masses terrifying,
their insidious destruction of lives unconscionable,
their hideous smirks hiding slyly,
seething behind black criss-cross lattice.

The Sun departs in orange-red flames,
darkness settles calmly
the horizon fading into night,
I throw the Tarot with hesitation
pondering the future.

THE DEVIL	THE TOWER	DEATH
☐	☐	☐
(past)	(present)	(future)

Arcanum Xlll, card of transformation
reveals the imminent transmutation of humanity
like mist rising from a valley of shadows,
absurd myths of the past forgotten,
absolute rein of the Three Religions is over
a triad of deceit, control and suffering
these edifices of deception self-disintegrating.

The Death card dominated by Scorpio
indicator of involuntary change,
death and rebirth from draconian ways
new life, new thought, new knowledge
renewed adoration of nature
reverence for her miraculous beauty,
the transformation bringing spiritual clarity
reinvigorating lives with wonder of the
Mysterium Tremendum et Fascinans.

The Perfect Fifth

… as I ascended the haunting harmonic scale
the archetype of the world came into view
like a miraculous omen,
graceful melodic breezes surrounded me
mauve with tinges of orange,
energies dancing in harmony
gently massaged my spirit.

… onward, further towards the celestial globe
glowing in golden brilliance,
I pondered the benevolent labours
the brilliance of homo sapiens,
counterpoint cut-deep, contrasting the evil
the stupidity and malicious malevolence.

… descending from the counterpoint censure
swirling downward like a swooping sea-bird
towards the planet veiled in turquoise-blue mist
nature glowed in her steadfast warmth
hinting at the possibility of a perfect existence,
the purity of eternal polyphony
pulsating for all to embrace
but understood by few,
we must rise again from the incarceration of darkness
to be entranced by the Music of the Spheres
and resonate with the Perfect Fifth.

Transcending the Quicksand

I struggle with tendrils of hatred
enveloping me like sticky spider web,
bruised by the lies spread mindlessly
the dark evil of the daily media
insidious,
infiltrating our lives and psyches,
deliberately and deviously.

I try to climb out of the quagmire
with head bowed attempt to pass by
the temptations of greed,
promises of the “good life”
promises of “eternal life”,
the tentacles mercilessly and unrelenting
keep dragging me into the foul quicksand,
the world an open bleeding wound.

Like Icarus I head towards the sun
only my wings are not wax,
but fashioned in golden threads of titanium
soaring through unknown dimensions
with shafts of light filtering through,
I realise transcending the morass
the foul mud created by human avarice
is the only possibility to avoid depression,
avoid feelings of impotence,
avoid thoughts of withdrawal,
to settle in a place of peace and harmony.

Grandma's Fruit Cake

Rising above the doctrine of fear,
no longer accepting the arrow of persecution
we move towards independence,
exposing Machiavellian mind control
clearing the dross of past ignorance
denouncing all deranged dictators,
new wisdom has been built from sorrow
dark valleys like the black heart of night
engulfing the innocent Everyman.

There is no - "stairway to heaven",
is no - "telephone to glory",
only a shimmering ladder to the stars
a ladder for all to climb,
the ladder is unsoiled
not stained with the blood of humiliation
the contamination of age-old suffering,
but you will need supplies on your journey,
an adventure to the heart of Eternity.

You could take -
"Some honey and plenty of money,
wrapped up in a five pound note!"
but more useful by far
old grandma's fruit cake,
her recipe ethereal and eternal,
even time travellers have to eat!

550gms flour
385gms currants
450gms raisins
500gms sultanas
80gms mixed peel
100gms glace cherries
85gms dates
1 cup rum
425gms butter
8 eggs
1 lemon rind
salt
bicarbonate of soda
2 cups brown sugar

The breeze reflects particles of oneness
as hearts reach for renewal,
fragrant purity gives way to flawless clarity
the sun of pure understanding shines intensely
with plumes of light cascading in harmony,
now the mind is content and overflowing,
Time for some fruit cake!

The Path

… fresh wounds from the mantle of nature
cut like a solipsistic nightmare,
a dreamscape-state with flecks of danger
agitating the coiled serpent,
a formidable protector
guarding the path to clarity.

Who dares to arouse the guardian?
Who dares to pass the sacred gatekeeper?

Arvo Pärt is roaring
an eloquent thundering,
the ancient forest vibrates to the tintinnabuli
deeper and deeper echoes taunt the moon
like shadows obscuring the truth,
an unspeakably sad melody follows the thunder,
rising, falling, pausing
cascading and stumbling over brown-black rocks.

I gaze hypnotically into the serpent's eye
time stands still as I merge with this ancient creature,
floating silently, moving slowly,
hovering like a drifting leaf
I pass unharmed
moving along the path to clarity.

The Hierophant

Part 1

The front door long gone
rusting hinges hang like omens,
climbing the old stairs cautiously
everywhere rotting boards
crumbling like the spirituality of humanity.

My eyes strain in the dimness
the moon's light insipid
fractured by the broken skylights above
the glass blackened by the cruelty of years,
everywhere danger surrounds me
each landing a respite from the climbing
each doorway a mysterious temptation.

"Enter at your own Risk" they seem to whisper,
scurrying and screeching chills my ears
the dark hallways harbingers of dread,
grasping the dark mahogany railing
its carving like a serpent's scales,
a false wish for security.

I climb towards the faltering light
"Look for the door with the Hierophant Carving",
shadows form and fade,
the last landing looms large
I startle a mouse with piercing eyes
darting towards a crack in the wall
it leaves me staring at the Hierophant!

Part 2

Ancient mystifying music enchants me
pulsing out from below the door,
it opens as I reach to knock,
an aged magi-like figure beckons,
heart pounding, I follow.

The long dark corridor, smoky
the fragrance of sandalwood intoxicating,
the magi opens the last door
entering the hallowed chamber
I am overwhelmed by the sanctity.

The Singing Bowls resonate,
their harmonies energise the air,

The Hierophant, surrounded by Tarot charts
arcane objects and pulsating orbs
directs me to a large cushion,
I sit at the centre of an ornate rug
a mandala with Major Arcana symbols,

"Be silent".

"Be still".

My passage begins.

Note From an Elder

Even the body meagre
ghastly, famished and cold
gently breathes in the prison of night,
it owes its existence to pure chance.

The hour hand moves slowly.

The tragedy unfolds each day,
stories and myths invented
every imaginable self-deception embraced,
the illusion of redemption
the illusion of salvation
the collusion of “the rapture”.

The hour hand moves a little faster.

The surge of time washes over,
rhythms of nature dance their dance
cyclic movements ebb and flow,
control and greed are idiot cousins
their characteristics wreaking havoc,
this miraculous planet is dying.

The hour hand is moving faster.

Indigenous peoples embrace ‘what is’,
symbiotic rapport with nature
no ‘town clocks’ to control and enslave
acceptance of limitations

harmonious empathy with daily cycles.
"No, we are not the pinnacle of evolution!"
"No, we cannot control earthquakes, cyclones and floods!"
"Yes, we flow with the flow of time!"
"We embrace the Tao!"

The hour hand is moving full-speed.

The Watch

I watch the glassy waters recede,
pulled towards the sea
relentless, silent.

Lady Luna smiles
her invisible force, irresistible
the daily, hourly movement
sketches time.

The ebb and flow
nature's timekeeper,
harbinger of civilization
ruler of romance
creator of cultures.

This incessant flow defines time,
like my great-grandfather's watch
150 years old keeping perfect time,
tick-tock, tick-tock, tick-tock
an ancient device from a forgotten era.

Bits of digital-gadgetry,
like a conjuror's illusion
fool us every day,
keeping us comatose,
pacifiers of harsh reality
and deceivers of the passage of time,
"Time and Tide wait for no one!"

Serpent Spirit

… thoughts can get caught on things
like spider web across the eyes,
trapped by invisible tendrils
like the unnoticed shackles of our minds.

… the mythical serpent rises
opening the entrance to the abyss of awe,
- swift as disaster,
- deliberate as retribution,
- incomprehensible as destiny.

… the serpent spirit lives on
surviving from the take over of Paganism,
A Universal Symbol of Heathen Idolatry!
deemed to be so by The Book of Deception
long after the transformation of Cadmus and Harmonia,
their transfiguration a sign for the bewildered
a light to illuminate the path of ignorance.

Digression - Memory Flash:
a sculpture carved by me in sandstone
towering – imposing – enigmatic
Moon God(dess) to celebrate the Luna lady
created with love and humility
offered to Gosford Shire
a gift for Rumbalara.
The sculptor is a Pagan Idolater!
cried the newspaper headline
deranged – disgusting,

Gosford Council, frightened, declined
terrified by the local Christian bullies.

...Heathen Idolatry – Pagan Idolater
my most cherished accolade!
Thank you!

...the spirit of the serpent lives on:
the Rainbow Spirit all seeing
directing the waters of our dry land,
the Ouroborous eternal
transformation, rebirth,
snakes intertwined around the Caduceus
symbol of the healing professions,
a symbol for printing,
a symbol for commerce.

Humans irrationally fear snakes
like they fear life and death
illogical, obsessive, misguided,
existential authenticity a vague dream.

A Promise

Part 1
I promised my friend I would visit her.
I had promised and promised and promised.
She probably did not believe I would ever
rcally visit her.
Clang clunk, clang/clunk the train
pulled out of another station. Clickty clack,
clickity clack, clickity clack. Speeding
along, faster, getting faster,faster,clickity
clack,clickity clack,clickityclack.
This train, this terrible trembling train
had tortured me too long. I decided to get off,
had to get off at the next station, next
station, next station. Didn't care where just had to get off,
had to get off, had to get off.
I got off. Ran down the platform, across
a dirt road, across a farmer's paddock, across
a bridge, across a creek. Running fast, fast,
running as fast as I could run.

Part 2
A way in the distance I saw a forest.
Had to get to the forest, had to, had to.
Running fast, faster,faster. The forest was
very close now, close,getting close,closer.
My heart was pounding fast, faster,faster,
thump/thump, thump/thump, thump/thump,
getting closer, thump/thump, thump/thump, my
legs were hurting, thump/thump, thump/thump.

The green-ness was soft, very soft. I
slowed to a walk, thump/thump, thump, thump,
slower, getting slower.
Tall tree ferns full of green-ness, full
of green softness surrounded me. Soothed me.
Delicate maiden hair nestled secure against a
weathered rock. A silent weathered rock.
Everything was calm, everything was still,
everything was soft, everything was silent.
My soft s - l - o - w breathing, silent,
still. Silent soft. I sank slowly onto the
silent weathered rock drifting into dreaming,
drowsy drifting, drifting, drifting.

Part3
When I awoke it was dark. Hiss-siss,
hiss-siss, hiss-siss, the strange noise was
getting louder. HISS-SISS, HISS-SISS. I jumped
up to run, HISS-SISS, HISS-SISS. Suddenly the
noise stopped. Now it was silent, not a
sound.
I needed to get out of this black dark-
ness, the gentle green-ness had turned to
frightening blackness. It curled around my
face and rubbed against my hand. Crash, the
twigs crushed under my step. Crash crash
crash crash. The crashing was deafening I
tried to walk softly. Quickly and softly.
I started running, running fast, faster
than I'd ever run, crashing, crunching through
bushes running faster. My heart was pounding
thump/thump, thump/thump,thump/thump, crashing
through cold grass, thump/thump, thump/thump,
thump/thump.

Part 4
A faint light appeared in the distance.
I slowed, slowed down, slowed to a walk.
My lungs hurt, bursting as I tried to grasp my
breath err/herr, err/herr, err herr, err
herr, err herr. My breathing
and walking were slowing, the light was getting
brighter and BRighter and BRIGHTER, then it
became two, there were smaller orange lights
following the searing white lights, it roared
past, THUNDERING the ground around me.
I didn't know where I was, couldn't
remember which station I'd left the train at.
I didn't know. I climbed up onto the
edge of the highway and started walking in the
direction of the disappearing lights.
The roadside gravel pushed up at my tired
feet, crunch, crunch, crunch, crunch. I was
getting hungry. Crunch, crunch, crunch,
crunch. My breathing was loud against the
still night air, ERR/HERR, ERR/HERR, ERR/HERR.
I walked on and on. I was very hungry.
Crunch, crunch, ERR/HERR, ERR/HERR, crunch,
crunch. The road was becoming steeper. The
walking was getting harder and slower, crunch,
crunch, crunch, crunch.
My breathing was getting harder and faster,
ERR/HERR, ERR/HERR ERRHERR ERRHERR
ERRHERR.

Part 5
Suddenly my eyes were glared by hundreds
of lights; street lights, coloured lights,

truck lights, shop lights. I saw a late night
cafe half-way down the hill. I started walking
faster, crunch, crunch,crunch,crunch,crunch my
hunger was overtaking me.
The fragrance of frying food and fresh
flowing coffee drew me to the cafe like a fly,
music cascaded out the door. "She loves you,
yeah, yeah, yeah. She loves you yeah, yeah,
yeah."
My hamburger oozed warm wetness down my
wrist, I sipped coffee, more hamburger, more
coffee, more hamburger.
Try some chicken, 'Flash'. Try some
chicken, 'Flash'. Try some chicken, 'Flash'.
The harshness, the cruelty of the neon flashing
seared my eyes. Three pieces of golden crumbed
chicken, gently fried chicken begged me to gulp
them down. Try some chicken 'Flash'. Try some
chicken, 'Flash'. My hunger was almost eaten
up as I chewed the last piece of chicken.

Part 6
Pain shot through my throat. Help!
Can't breathe. Help! Can't breathe.
The music faded with the lights. Spinning
fading, pulsating. My ears were buzzing,
bezzz, bezzz, bezzz. My head was exploding
boom/boom, boom/boom, boom/boom. Spinning,
spinning, falling, drifting into dreaming,
drifting, drifting, drifting, drifting.

Part 7
White-ness surrounded me everywhere,
white-ness, white uniforms, white sheets, white

walls. A trolley with red all over the white
hurtled past the white door. Click/clack,
patter/patter, click/clack, patter/patter,
getting faster, click/clack,patter/patter,
clickclack patterpatter clickclackpatterpatter.
"Paging Nurse Green!" "Paging Nurse
Green!" "Emergency!" "Emergency!" Click/clack
patter/patter, click/clack, patter/patter.
"Paging Nurse Green!" "Paging Nurse Green!"
"Emergency!" "Emergency!"
I sat up grasping my throat, I could feel
the pain inside, my breath rasped, gerr/gherr,
gerr/gherr, gerr/gherr, gerr/gherr. My head
sank back into the soft white-ness of the
pillow. Every time I set out to visit my
friend something like this happens, but she
never believes me.

Homeward Bound

From the dark belligerent nightly news
a hopeless sense of misery engulfs me,
exploding forth with cyclonic fury
memories enshrined in my heart, agitated
like dead leaves jostled by a restless wind.

Then a spark of hope arises in my despair,
the sandstone and eucalypt hills surround me
yellow-red ancient stones
contrast the soft green trees
guarding and guiding the sacred river,
a silent place!

A sanctuary for a reclusive life,
the spirit of this Hawkesbury rift incessant,

"return to your ancestral home"
spirits beckon
"return to the hearth of creation".

This is Darug-Darkinjung country
a place where the tides dominate,
the pulse and flow
a connection to unknown realms,
deep-water reflects rocky outcrops
dense mangroves,
the roots gnarled and tangled
bathe in the shallow liminal zone.

Sunrise paints a surreal scene
blazing orange-red cascades down the valley
reflecting image-perfect from the still-mirror-river
a new day has arrived in mesmerising splendour.

Serenity – Silence – Seclusion – Stillness
surround me.

I am home!

Sorting Archetypes

... travelling easily in the Quantum vacuum
I sort and arrange archetypes,
some older than time
some evolving to resonate with new myths.

the universe breaths in
the universe breaths out,
galaxies grow to perfection
galaxies decay disappearing into dark matter,
an abundance of dimensions interact
some accessible to our tiny minds
some remain forever illusive.

travelling slower I approach my limitations,
I accept these limits of unknowing
I marvel at the miracle of conscious awareness.

Sea of Light

the envious moon locked in a never ending cycle
a winged messenger of unbroken wholeness
taunts the lazy pacing clouds,
illuminating rivers and mountains
shadowing the forgotten ancestor spirits,
numerous dimensions ebb and flow
dancing in natural sympathy
through the Universal Sea of Light.

Wandjina walked the Earth
making ALL from the mysterious void
transforming cosmological harmonics into sacred sites,
gifting the miracle of the First Fire,
creating the Dreaming to guide humans,
Tiddalick the Frog ....
sharing resources, the only sustainable way.
Emu and Jabiri ....
co-operation, the only survival possibility.

Wandjina is weeping!

In Stillness

the relentless wandering eye
penetrated my secret thoughts
like the silent stealth of a cat,
and then the quiet descended
the stillness carried me away
a glimpse of darkness
silence .... calm.

Shadows danced rhythmically
as the night birds watched silently
charcoal ..... black
dissolved into grey,
the utter loneliness of the night penetrating
caressing my melancholia with apprehension
I gazed into my own shadow
a tangled shifting puzzle of doubt.

Descend to the mirrored water
a voice full of confidence
commanded me relentlessly,
the dense mangroves danced in the reflection,
the night birds sang softly,
overlapping circles of tidal-flow
caressed the mangrove roots.

All was still
all was as it should be,
I glimpsed the key to eternity.

Quantum Vagrancy At The Shop

The illusory nature of inexorable change
with symmetry building ability
has reached a temporal facet of its existence,
spontaneous emergence of archetypal imagery
with self-similar iterations sadly collapses,
creation of oppressive deconstruction evolution
questions the maturity of quantum vagrancy.

The shopper is deeply entangled,
trapped between the shopping-list-lines;
500 grams pumpkin
one dozen eggs
two litres of white vinegar
ten packets of black jelly beans
100 grams Darjeeling tea
one packet split, black, French lentils.

The dawn of the background sea of light
reaching a temporal facet of being
far into the aminergic-cholinergic system
has caused a higher dimensional phase-space,
a place to hang your hat
a place to call home
a place where no one can intrude.

Do not forget to put rum in the fruit cake.

Connected everywhere and nowhere brings confusion,
spinning through the sixth dimension

travelling fast, travelling alone
the great perturbations of Brahman's breath
crash the infallible systems of control,
the illusory deceptions of the oldest symbols
— in cyclic return —
have become strange attractors.

The shopper is now hopelessly entangled;
93120813 Metal Paint Aerosol 350g $19.90
93006124 British Paints P&P spray $8.30
93155707 Everhang Picture wire $3.68
Subtotal $31.88
Total $31.88
(GST included)

Grandma suggested salt is a good stain remover
rugs, shirt fronts, socks,
all will respond to the treatment,
slightly dampened, left for five minutes.

The alchemical treatise *De Lapide Philisophico*
heralds the dawn of archetypes,
the symbols of unbroken wholeness,
And Grandma agrees!

Sliced Bread

... "the best thing since sliced bread"

we use the saying from time to time mindlessly,
bread is a tasty metaphor for life,
uttering, "the best thing since sliced bread"
we are honouring uniformity, sterility and tastelessness,
a non-thinking progress monger invented sliced bread
returning humankind towards our beginnings in the primeval swamp.

the tongue is an incredibly sensitive, complex piece of evolution,
the practice of "breaking bread' wasn't because thieves stole the cutlery,
because the surface of broken bread becomes uneven,
cover this uneven surface with butter, gravy or honey
(I bet you're feeling hungry now)
some thick areas, some thin, perhaps some areas with no topping at all
rolling down the hills and valleys of life's metaphor,
the human tongue loves subtle variations.

mercilessly mechanically sliced bread has the surface smooth and even,
topping is spread in a thin, uneventful slime
force this into your mouth against nature's discretion
your trembling tongue thinks how boring!
just like modern life if you don't guard against being programmed,
coded into a uniform, sterile profitability orientated,
square tomato prioritised society.

Cutting bread is not intrinsically wrong
it's how it's cut that's the dilemma,
manually sliced bread ends up thicker at one end,
pulled a bit in the centre,
rougher on the surface,
all subtle topographical features enhancing the taste.

not yet convinced of these words of wisdom
takc your piece of rough sawn bread and toast it!
Wow.
Now you not only have all the hills and valleys,
some charred, some golden brown and some warm
words can no longer capture the exquisite orgasmic rapture.

ever wondered why white bread became so popular,
we are brain washed into believing everything, everything
white and unblemished is pure and God like
(an absurd heresy),
whole grain, real bread is difficult to mechanically slice
it doesn't end up perfectly uniform
the non-thinking manufacturers assumed this would match their
customers personalities,
Big mistake MR Sliced Bread,
the next revolution will be, "The Anti-Sliced Bread Revolution".

Shades of Shadows

I grasp their identities
as I sit on a decaying cane chair
weaving an inner story of hope,
developing layers of transient lives
exploring the mysteries of shadows.

The dark firmament penetrates the depths
where magic once in the heart has faded,
it drifts past me in unanswered questions
floating across the night in black silence.

Why have these lives disintegrated
collapsed in hopeless despair?
the homeless sleep rough,
subsisting on the discards of affluence.

When they do - “go gentle into that good night”
I wonder who ever feels remorse or even cares?

Archeus

...for fire tests everything...

from within the fire transcendence occurs
transmutation beyond anthropocentrism becomes possible,
the green transparent Chrysoprasus may emerge
the black crystal through Spagyria pulsates
but these are not The Stone.

Sacred letters of the world confuse the ignorant
anthropocentric attachments deceive with blackness
locking us into three dimensions of enslavement.
Rectores Mundorum's wisdom resonates subtly
gently caressing the waves of being,

Freedom to explore unimaginable realms open
through the purifying essence of fire,
slowly multi-dimensional reality appears.

NB:
Archeus – vital principle enabling life
Rectorus Mundorum – divine regents mentioned in the Chaldean oracles
Spagyria – method of preparing alchemical medicines

Bundjulahm (Revisited)

The turtles swim in circles
high in the headwaters of the Clarence River,
Bundjulahm once dived to catch them,
then she painted them.
Stories of childhood she relates brightly
remembering the carefree happy times
reminding me her name means, *Butterfly*.

The Bundjalung elder paints for love
caressing the colours of her sacred land,
dots and dots and circles within circles
the turtles swim and dive serenely.

Now the carefree times are gone
her wheel chair keeps her mobile,
dialysis keeps her alive day-after-day,
a life shortened by a deadly-white-diet
consequences beyond ignorance
beyond the mindlessness of holier-than-thou missionaries,
miraculously she still laughs and sings.

Recently she rejoined her ancestor spirits
to paint the land into being
from a different vantage.

NB: The Bundjalung people are Australian Aborigines who are the original custodians of a the land from Grafton on the north coast of New South Wales to Beaudesert in south-east Queensland. Bundjulahm, aka Patsy Nagas, was a Bundjalung elder.

No Fish Again!

The Last Manifesto of an Ageing Cynical Artist

i went fishing today .....
for the last time!
illusions drifted away
purged by the howling southerly,
no fish again!

unrealistic dreams finally discarded,
poetry and art does not change the world
poetry and art cannot change the world.
"Come you Masters of War",
still wars and hatred rage;
"Imagine living life in peace",
still wars and hatred rage;
"Guernica" a masterpiece of global renown,
still wars and hatred rage;
"Alchemy", Whitley's tour de force
his illusion it would end a war,
still the war and hatred raged.

words and works known by millions
impotent and useless tools of change,
my pathetic poetic pleas for peace
known by few, what chance?
the illusion has drifted away.

Spring Arts Festival in Nimbin
my last art show!

What hate filled god,
what evil curse of Saturn
implanted this creative impulse?
a desire to make the world a better place for all.
half a century of futility
how could I be so gullible and foolish?
my father told me I was thus many years ago
I laughed.
the joke is on the poet,
the egg is on this artist's face.

"I don't need a reason
For what I became
I've got these excuses
They're tired and lame
don't need a pardon
There's no one left to blame
I'm leaving the table
I'm out of the game." (Leonard Cohen)

Now!

Now – *"time is not on my side"*

No explanations,
No reasons,
No philosophy,
No art-speak stun-gun hype,

Mysterium Tremendum et Fascinans
is all there is!

Other books written, edited or co-edited by Robert Maddox-Harle (aka Rob Harle)

Searching For The Sublime: Poems from Australia & India (ed. Jaydeep Sarangi & Rob Harle) Cyberwit, India. (2016)
Homeward Bound: Poems from Australia & India (ed. Jaydeep Sarangi & Rob Harle) Cyberwit, India. (2015)
The Land: Poems from Australia & India (ed. Jaydeep Sarangi & Rob Harle) Cyberwit, India. (2015)
PCK Prem Echoing Time and Civilisations (ed. Harle, Sharma & Sharma) Authorspress, India. (2015)
Indo-Australian Anthology of Short Fiction (ed. Harle, Sharma & Sharma) Authorspress, India. (2014)
Voices Across Generations: Poetry Past & Present (ed. Rob Harle) Authorspress, India. (2014)
Voices Across The Ocean: Poems from Australia & India (ed. Rob Harle & Jaydeep Sarangi) Cyberwit, India. (2014)
Indo-Australian Anthology of Contemporary Poetry (ed. Sharma, Harle & Sharma) Authorspress, India. (2013)
Building Bridges: Poems from Australia & India (ed. Rob Harle) Cyberwit, India. (2013)
The Clock by Diane Hosking (ed. Rob Harle) Spinning Spider Publications, Australia. (2004)
Scratches & Deeper Wounds Poetry by Rob Harle Spinning Spider Publications, Australia. (1996)
Mechanisms Of Desire Poetry by Rob Harle Spinning Spider Publications, Australia. (2012)
Winds of Infinity Poetry by Rob Harle Cyberwit, India. (2016)
The Blazing Furnace an eclectic collection of experimental poems with images
Robert Maddox-Harle Cyberwit, India. (2022)

www.ingramcontent.com/pod-product-compliance
Ingram Content Group UK Ltd.
Pitfield, Milton Keynes, MK11 3LW, UK
UKHW041316190726
13845UKWH00025B/300

9 789363 546882